25 Mind Mapping Strategies For Women with Adult ADHD

Proven Daily Brain exercise and Guide to Stay Focused for a Positive Transformation, Improve Relationship and Manage Your Emotion and Thoughts to Become Productive

Courtney L. Swenson

All rights reserved. No part of this publication may be reproduced, distributed, or transmitted in any form or by any means, including photocopying, recording, or other electronic or mechanical methods, without the prior written permission of the publisher, except in the case of brief quotations embodied in critical reviews and certain other noncommercial uses permitted by copyright law.

THIS ARE THE MIND MAPPING STRATEGIES FOR WOMEN WITH ADHD

INTRODUCTION

An urban legend tells the tale of **Sarah**, a woman who lived in a city filled with towering buildings and crowded streets. Due to her history of coping with adult ADHD and PTSD, Sarah had encountered challenges earlier in life. Every day seemed like an uphill struggle since her mind was like a turbulent sea of ideas and feelings.

As **Sarah** sat at her disorganized desk, consumed by mental chaos, one fateful evening, she stumbled onto a process called mind mapping. **Sarah**, captivated by the idea of order and precision, decided to embark on an experimental adventure armed only with a pen and some blank paper.

When **Sarah** began to put her thoughts and ideas on paper, a rush of relaxation washed over her. It was as if her thoughts were slowly beginning to make sense of everything, revealing connections and paths she had never considered before. She found her way out of the dark tunnel of her mind with each stroke of her pen, which was like a beacon of light.

As Sarah continued to expand her mind map, she began to feel more and more capable. Instead of being a victim of her overwhelming emotions and thoughts, she took charge of her life and made a strategy for understanding and clarity.

Sarah uncovered twenty distinct methods intended exclusively for women who battle with adult ADHD and PTSD through the power of mind mapping. Every strategy, from increasing memory and recall to visualizing ideas and thoughts, was a step toward a better, more ordered future.

Sarah couldn't help but feel happy and successful as she stared down at her finished mind map. Her ability to turn what had earlier been a jumbled mix of ideas into a skillfully arranged work of art is evidence of her perseverance and courage.

So, empowered with her newfound insight and a rejuvenated sense of purpose, Sarah set out to tackle the hurdles that lay ahead, knowing that she could gracefully and decisively manage the complexities of her own mind.

Drawing a bright map of your thoughts and emotions, with each notion related to other ideas like highways on a map, is what mind mapping resembles. You can convey how you feel with graphics, colors, and symbols rather of only putting things down in a list. It's like having a specific tool to assist make sense of the tangle of ideas and emotions in your head for ladies experiencing adult **ADHD** and **PTSD**.

ENJOY YOUR SERIES

~STRATEGY 1~

---

*T*hink about mind mapping as a technique to

organize the puzzle pieces in your mind so they make sense. First, you set your key thought, analogous to the beginning of a journey, in the center of the map. You then draw lines that branch out from that point, including numerous emotions and thoughts as you proceed.

The map's branches can each stand for a separate concept, such as an idea, emotion, or memory. Furthermore, these branches can occasionally link in unexpected ways, just like in real life. This can assist you in seeing the links between your thoughts and feelings.

The adaptability of mind mapping is its best feature. You can move objects, add new branches, and adjust the color at any time. It's analogous to being an artist in your own thoughts, drawing a gorgeous portrait of your emotions and ideas.

Additionally, as you work on your mind map, you may begin to see connections and patterns that you were previously unaware of. This can assist you in establishing a greater self-awareness and coping technique for tough emotions.

Start with a key Theme: To get started, determine which significant issue or key theme you desire to examine. This might be a particular mood, a target you'd like to attain, or an issue you're dealing with.

Use Colors and Symbols: To symbolize distinct feelings, concepts, or categories, use colors and symbols in your mind map. Use cold tones like blue or green to depict tranquil or cheerful attitudes, and warm hues like red or orange to indicate powerful emotions.

Branch Out: To illustrate related ideas or subtopics, build branches that radiate from the main theme. Your ideas are structured logically in a hierarchical framework where each branch could lead to other branches.

Add Keywords and Short Phrases: To convey the core idea of your writing, apply keywords or short phrases in place of lengthy paragraphs. As a result, the map is simple and succinct at a glance.

Include Visuals and Images: To boost your mind map's visual appeal, include visuals such as icons, symbols, or images that speak to you. Images have the potential to stimulate sentiments and strengthen intellectual relationships.

Connect concepts: To represent the flow of thinking or to connect related concepts, use lines or arrows. This illustrates how many concepts relate to one another and highlights how your ideas are interconnected.

Try Different Layouts: Investigate many combinations to find which one suits you the best. While some people like a more linear or organic arrangement, others could prefer a radial pattern with the principal theme at the middle and branches spreading outward.

Review and Consider: Every now and then, go back over your mind map and consider the connections you've drawn. This can help you obtain a deeper understanding of your feelings and ideas and bring out areas that might require additional in-depth examination or assistance.

- **1.1 MIND MAPPING TECHNIQUES**

Using mind mapping to picture ideas and thoughts is similar to constructing a lively mental tale. Rather than putting down your thoughts in a dry list, you may describe your sentiments using drawings and colors. This strategy can be a game-changer for women who are battling with adult ADHD and PTSD.

Imagine your mind as a wide, unfettered environment where ideas are free to flow. You can write down your thoughts by employing mind mapping, which is analogous to constructing an internal map of your mind. It's similar to making a visual journal where you can view all of your thoughts in one location.

Using digital mind mapping tools such as **MindMeister or SimpleMind** is analogous to having an infinitely huge magic canvas. You can make as many branches as you like, zoom in and out, and express your emotions with different colors. It is akin to utilizing your thoughts to paint a picture.

You may see relationships between concepts as you work on your mind map. Perhaps one concept inspires another, much like tracing a path through a forest with breadcrumbs. This can assist you in better comprehending your thoughts and organizing your sentiments.

Your mind map's branches each stand for individual ideas or concepts, and the nodes themselves are analogous to small inspiration sparks. You can use symbols and pictures to visually convey your ideas, or you can add words or phrases to communicate your thoughts and feelings.

The fact that mind mapping is rule-free is its best feature. You can use your creativity to build a map that is as distinct as you are. Mind mapping is a process that can help you express yourself and make sense of your ideas and feelings, regardless of how you're feeling—happy, unhappy, bewildered, or delighted.

- **1.2 Visualizing Thoughts and Ideas**

Effectively organizing knowledge with mind mapping is equivalent to constructing a customized road map for traversing the complexity of your own mind. This strategy can be an effective means of achieving attention in the midst of confusion for women living with adult **ADHD and PTSD**.

Think of your mind as a busy metropolis, full of ideas and thoughts that are racing through it like traffic on a busy roadway. Mind mapping gives an organized way for classifying and arranging ideas, which helps generate order in this hectic city.

The numerous branches inside the mind map symbolize distinct characteristics of your ideas or encounters, analogous to routes leading to various regions. You can build a passage across the mental maze that is both clear and well-organized by positioning these branches strategically.

Like finding hidden jewels lying beneath the surface, you may find deeper connections and insights as you examine your thoughts. You may learn more about yourself and your experiences via this highly empowering process of inquiry and discovery.

You are organizing information with each branch you add to your mind map, but you are also developing a visual image of your inner world. And as your map takes shape, you'll realize that what at first appeared to be a jumbled mix of ideas has evolved into a masterfully constructed work of art, which is a testament to your determination and bravery.

~STRATEGY 2~

Brain Exercises Every Day

Our minds frequently absorb the brunt of life's turbulent journey, particularly for individuals with adult ADHD and PTSD. Daily brain workouts appear as a light of hope for mental health, presenting a road map for resilience and clarity.

Let's analyze three essential methods that belong within this group:

★ **2.1. Mindfulness and Meditation Techniques:**

Imagine a peaceful oasis of tranquility where the mind can find calmness and consolation among the daily bustle. The portal to this inner sanctuary is opened by mindfulness and meditation techniques, which assist people to acquire a strong sense of awareness and presence.

The route to inner tranquility for those with adult ADHD and PTSD may resemble traversing a tumultuous sea of sensations and ideas. They can, however, learn to center themselves in the here and now and escape the raging rivers of their minds by engaging in mindfulness and meditation activities.

They experience a wave of calmness that settles their strained nerves and silences their minds' incessant chatter as they close their eyes and concentrate on their breathing. They embrace tranquility and release stress with every breath, enabling themselves to truly experience the richness of the present moment.

People with adult ADHD and PTSD can develop resilience in the face of hardship by practicing persistently, and they can learn to handle the ups and downs of their thoughts and emotions with love and grace. Mindfulness and meditation become more than just mental workouts; they become excellent instruments for self-healing and self-discovery.

★ **awareness and meditation practices;**

Close your eyes and either lie down or sit comfortably to practice body scan meditation. Gradually transfer your focus to various body locations, beginning with your toes and going up to your head. With each exhale, allow yourself to release any tension or tightness in the affected areas or sensations.

Select a modest serving of food, such an apple slice or a raisin, and practice mindful eating. Spend some time evaluating the meal with all of your senses before you consume it; take note of its color, texture, and fragrance.

Chew on a tiny piece at a time, examining the texture and flavor as you go. Without passing judgment, take note of any thoughts or feelings that surface and return your focus back to the here and now.

2.2 Activities for Cognitive Stimulation

Think of the mind as a muscle that gets stronger and more resilient when it is trained; a muscle that thrives on activity. A wide range of exercises meant to stimulate and challenge the brain, enhance mental agility and cognitive flexibility, are supplied by cognitive stimulation activities.

Cognitive stimulation activities can be likened to an exciting tour of exploration and discovery through the vast landscape of the mind for persons with adult ADHD and PTSD. Engaging in puzzles, brain teasers, strategic games, and creative hobbies stimulates the brain and encourages the formation and development of neural connections.

Engaging in these activities helps people feel thrilled and curious, which makes them desire to explore new pathways of thought and widen their cognitive boundaries. They become more self-assured and have a better awareness of their cognitive skills and weaknesses with every challenge they overcome.

Regular engagement in cognitive stimulation exercises builds emotional resilience in addition to enhanced cognitive function, giving people the tools they need to boldly and clearly handle life's problems. They come out of each activity stronger, smarter, and more resilient than before, much like an experienced navigator finding a course through unknown waters.

Practices for Cognitive Stimulation Activities

☐ **Crossword puzzles**: Test your vocabulary and problem-solving talents by taking on crossword puzzles. As you grow better, work your way up to increasingly harder difficulties. Playing crossword puzzles enhances your language and cognitive skills while also engaging your brain.

Play strategy games like chess or others that call for planning, intelligence, and fast thinking. These games not only occupy your mind but also help you become more adept at anticipating and responding to varied situations, which enhances your cognitive flexibility and ability to make judgments.

☐ **Learning a New talent:** Take up a new interest-driven activity or talent, like painting, playing an instrument, or taking up a language. Learning and mastering a new ability puts your brain under pressure to alter and evolve, which fosters cognitive resilience and neural plasticity.

~STRATEGY 3~

Strategies for Positive Transformation

★ **Exercise to Promote Mental Clarity:**
Exercise turns up as a significant catalyst for mental clarity and emotional well-being in the dance of mind and body. Including regular physical activity in one's daily routine can be a transformational practice for persons with adult ADHD and PTSD, providing a comprehensive approach to resilience and brain health.

Adult ADHD and PTSD sufferers go on a trip of physical exercise and mental regeneration when they lace up their sneakers and step outside into the cold morning air. They become anchored in the present moment and clear and declutter their minds with every step they take because they can feel the steady beat of their heart and the rhythmic cadence of their breath.

Physical activity, whether it be an intense cardio workout, a soothing yoga session, or a leisurely stroll around the park, functions as a trigger for emotional and mental stability. They feel a deep sense of energy and well-being as endorphins flood their system and tension melts away, leaving them energetic and focused to take on the duties of the day.

People with adult ADHD and PTSD who exercise consistently develop resilience and fortitude in the face of suffering by strengthening their bodies and feeding their minds. They are laying the road for a more hopeful and active future by improving psychologically and emotionally with every step they take in the direction of improved physical health.

★ **Exercise to Promote Mental Clarity:**

Walking or Jogging: Go for a brisk stroll or a run through your community or a local park. Engaging in physical activity boosts blood circulation to the brain, stimulating the creation of neurotransmitters and endorphins that improve mood and mental performance. As you move your body, become entirely present in the moment by focusing on the sights, sounds, and sensations around you.

Exercise yoga or tai chi: These kinds of exercise combine deliberate breathing, gentle movement, and attention to detail. These mind-body strategies assist relaxation, boost focus, and minimize stress and anxiety. Release tension and distractions as you flow through each posture or sequence, focussing exclusively on the feel of your breath and your body's movement.

Dancing or Aerobic training: Play your choice music and either dance in your living room or take part in an aerobic training session. In addition to boosting cardiovascular health, dancing and aerobic exercise allow endorphins to be released, which enhances mood and boosts focus. Move freely and expressively, releasing tension and stress with each motion. Techniques for Positive Transformation

3.1. Finding Coping Strategies and Triggers:

Finding your coping skills and triggers is like turning on a spotlight in the shadowy parts of your mind to see what's upsetting or overwhelming and how to handle it. It's akin to fitting the pieces of a puzzle together after you know where they go; that way, everything makes sense.

This road could seem scary for women who are suffering from Adult ADHD and PTSD, but it's also empowering since it offers you the capacity to take responsibility of your feelings and responses.

Finding your triggers is basically discovering out what makes you feel stressed, anxious, or other undesirable emotions. Anything from certain circumstances or locations to particular ideas or memories can function as a trigger. You can begin to comprehend why you feel the way you do in particular circumstances and take action to manage your reactions by being aware of these triggers.

Contrarily, coping strategies are the ways and tactics you adopt to handle those triggers and the feelings they generate. These might varied considerably from person to person and could be as simple as taking a break, talking to a friend, or engaging in mindfulness activities. Finding coping skills that work for you is crucial, as is practicing them regularly until they come effortlessly.

For instance, if you are aware that crowded settings make you uncomfortable, you may learn to deal by keeping headphones on hand so you can listen to podcasts or relaxing music when you're out in public. Alternatively, if you realize that specific memories or thoughts consistently make you feel melancholy or angry, you might utilize tools like journaling or cognitive behavioral therapy to help you cope with those feelings in a healthy way.

• **Seeking Professional Guidance**

If you're having difficulties with trauma or ADHD, you might want to talk to a therapist or counselor. To aid you in recognizing triggers, processing emotions, and building coping mechanisms that are relevant to your requirements, a professional can offer tailored advice and therapeutic approaches.

Creating a network of persons who support you is like having a group of people who are always there for you. It's akin to constructing a safety net of dependable people—friends, family, and other—who will catch you when you fall and give you a hand up when you need it most.

It is vital for women who are struggling with adult **ADHD** and **PTSD** to have a robust support network. It includes surrounding yourself with others who are sympathetic to your position and who are available to provide a sympathetic ear, a shoulder to grieve on, or valuable aid when needed. Having an encouraging network may be highly beneficial, whether you need someone to chat to about your troubles, assist you with ordinary duties, or just sit with you in silence.

You may feel confident speaking up to trusted family members or close friends as part of your support system. It might also incorporate internet forums or support groups where you can engage with folks going through analogous conditions. Finding friends that you can rely on for assistance at difficult times and who help you feel understood and welcomed is vital.

Although developing a supporting network needs time and commitment, the rewards are priceless. It not only gives you practical support and emotional support, but it also helps fight against feelings of loneliness and isolation that are usually associated with mental health difficulties.

Make a connection with your peers by contacting online forums or support groups for ladies who suffer from PTSD and ADHD. Feeling less alone and more supported on your road can be achieved by sharing experiences and views with people who are familiar with your position.

Lean on Loved Ones: Seek out emotional support and encouragement from friends, family, or trustworthy loved ones. Talk to someone about your needs and concerns, and be open to accept support when it is given. During hard situations, having solid ties with loved ones can bring one a sense of stability and belonging.

Professional Support: If you're looking for treatment with trauma and ADHD, think about working with a therapist or coach. A professional may provide guidance, validation, and practical suggestions on how to handle interpersonal situations and develop a solid support system.

3.3. Acquiring Self-Acceptance and Compassion:

It's akin to treating yourself with care and understanding even when you're going through problems or setbacks: cultivating self-compassion and acceptance. It's like having a soothing companion instead of a harsh critic for oneself.

This strategy entails teaching women with adult ADHD and PTSD how to embrace and acknowledge their own feelings and experiences without passing judgment or blaming themselves. It's about acknowledging that, like everyone else, you deserve compassion and understanding and that it's acceptable to struggle and make blunders.

recognizing and being compassionate toward oneself entails recognizing your shortcomings as well as your essential worth as a person. It's about learning to accept yourself for who you are, in spite of situations that don't work out the way you had hoped.

It can be challenging to follow this path of self-acceptance and compassion, particularly for women who have undergone trauma or battle mental health difficulties. It demands for endurance, bravery, and a preparedness to face hard sensations and ideas. However, in the end, it can result in substantial healing and transformation, supporting women in creating a deeper feeling of empowerment and self-love.

Practice Self-Kindness: Show yourself the same care and consideration that you would show a good friend. Without passing judgment, embrace your struggles and hardships and give yourself words of support and encouragement.

Defy Negative Self-Talk: Be conscious of your inner talk and challenge any self-deprecating or negative notions that come up. Remind yourself of your innate worth and resilience by substituting positive self-talk with declarations of self-love and acceptance.

Finding techniques to manage powerful emotions of concern, anxiety, or uneasiness is vital to control worried thoughts. This can be particularly tough for adults with adult ADHD and PTSD. These approaches allow people a sense of control over their moods and responses, which enhances their capacity to manage daily life.

Your mind can feel like a cyclone when you're anxious, which makes it difficult to concentrate or feel at ease. But you can calm the storm and feel more at ease if you can learn to control them.

Anxious thoughts can be particularly challenging for persons with **ADHD** and **PTSD** to handle since these conditions may produce aberrant brain function that makes it more difficult to control emotions. However, they can adopt coping methods to feel more in command.

Envision yourself in a boat on a turbulent sea. Feeling wobbly and enduring waves of worry are analogous to huge waves that shake your boat. However, you may choose calmer waters and learn to sail your boat through waves provided you have the right equipment.

People can learn to relax and take back control of their thoughts and emotions by adopting these tactics. It's akin to learning how to manage a ship through terrible seas with power and confidence as the captain.

~STRATEGY 4~

CONTROLLING ANXIOUS THOUGHTS

4.1. Cognitive-Behavioral Methods:

The purpose of cognitive-behavioral treatments is to identify and address the negative ideas that generate anxiety. It's as like you're illuminating those thoughts and proving to yourself that they're not always right.

This is how it happens: Occasionally, our ideas fool us into thinking things that aren't exactly accurate or equitable. These concepts have the ability to induce significant anxiety. However, we can begin to feel less apprehensive and more at ease by learning to question those ideas and evaluate things from a different perspective.

Consider this: You are staring at a painting that has had a dark filter applied to it, causing everything to appear dismal. You may perceive the picture in its actual hues, which can be more brighter and more positive, when you remove the filter with the use of cognitive-behavioral techniques.

Practice tasks:

- **Thought Tracking**:

Write down all of your worrying thoughts during the day in a journal. Take notice of the conditions or triggers that create these views, and evaluate the arguments for and against them. Subsequently, refute incorrect beliefs by introducing more constructive and reasonable concepts.

- **Relaxation Techniques**

: To relieve physical tension and increase relaxation, consider progressive muscle relaxation or guided visualization. These hobbies can aid in lowering anxiety symptoms and creating inner calm.

Exposure therapy includes systematically and increasingly exposing oneself to triggers or experiences that create fear. Work your way up to more challenging situations by starting with ones that bring you less stress. With time, this exposure can assist in decreasing your overall anxiety levels and desensitizing you to stimuli that cause worry.

4.2. Relaxation Breathing Exercises:

When you are feeling worried, breathing exercises are like hitting the reset button for your body and mind. These are straightforward approaches that employ your attention to the breath to help you relax.

This is how it happens: Anxious sensations lead your mind to race with tension-inducing worries and thoughts. Breathing techniques assist you in redirecting your attention from those notions to your breathing. You may relax your thoughts and unwind your body by breathing deeply and gently, focusing on each inhalation and exhale.

It's equivalent to taking a deep breath of fresh air after withdrawing from a busy street. Breathing in allows you to fill your lungs with peace, while exhaling allows you to relieve tension and stress.

Practice tasks:

Deep Breathing: To engage in deep breathing exercises, slowly inhale deeply through your nose and let your abdomen expand entirely. After holding the breath for a brief while, slowly expel the air from your mouth to empty your lungs totally. Several times over, repeat this method while paying attention to how your breath enters and exits your body.

Try the 4-7-8 breathing technique, which is four counts of inhalation, seven counts of holding the breath, and eight counts of exhale. This rhythm promotes profound relaxation and helps to balance the neurological system.

Breath Counting: As you inhale and exhale, sit quietly and count each breath. As you inhale, count to one, as you exhale, count to two, and so on until you reach ten. Just go back to one and start over if you lose track or get diverted. This technique helps relaxation and mental focus.

4.3. Using a Journal to Let Go of Fears:

Through the therapeutic practice of journaling, people can securely and nonjudgmentally share their ideas and experiences. People can obtain clarity and insight into their feelings and externalize their fears by putting pen to paper.

Practice tasks:

Stream-of-Consciousness Writing: Allocate a period of time each day for unrestrained writing. Don't think about punctuation or grammar; simply write what comes to mind. This method can help the catharsis and release of repressed feelings.

- **Gratitude Journaling**:

 List three things, no matter how tiny, for which you are thankful each day. By focused on the positive aspects of your life, you can generate a sense of appreciation and well-being and shift your attitude.

- **Worry Journal**:

Start a worry journal in which you can record any anxious ideas or feelings that come up during the day. After you've recorded them, schedule some time to go over and take care of them later. This practice can boost problem-solving and assist to avoid rumination.

~STRATEGY 5~

Improving Focus and Concentration

Enhancing concentration and focus is essential for both general well-being and productivity. It's critical to establish a space that reduces distractions, practice time management, and make use of technological tools in order to do this.

Let's examine each in more detail:

★ Establishing a Distraction-Free Environment:

Diversions can impair focus and reduce output. Establish a designated workstation that is noise- and clutter-free to counteract this. Clear the area of any possible distractions, such as electronics or background noise, and establish a relaxing environment that will help you concentrate.

Establish limits and share them with others to reduce disruptions when working or studying.

Practice tasks:

Assign a particular spot in your house or place of business as your devoted workspace. Make sure everything is organized and devoid of anything that could distract you.

Establish limits with family members or roommates to reduce disruptions when working or studying.

To reduce noise and create a calm atmosphere, use white noise generators or noise-canceling headphones.

18 work-related time management techniques

The time management techniques listed below might help you become more productive at work and manage your time better.

1. Plan your day before it begins.

Everything begins with a plan. You should make a plan for everything you want to get done that day in order to use your time wisely.

Making a to-do list of everything you need and want to get done is the simplest approach to start organizing your workday.

While creating a to-do list isn't a novel approach, it can significantly improve how efficiently you manage your time throughout the day.

"Make sure to physically cross off items from your to-do list as you do them to give yourself a sense of satisfaction and to be able to look back and see what you accomplished that day."

2. Set the most crucial tasks first.

It is now time to prioritize your to-do list after you have built it. Setting priorities enables you to focus on the most crucial tasks of the day and make efficient use of your time.

There are numerous methods for ranking the items on your to-do list in order of importance.

Decide which three tasks are the most critical for you to do and begin going.

Divide your duties into three priority categories: high, medium, and low.

in a scale of 1 to 10, rank each item in your list, and then arrange them in that order.

3. Break up bigger jobs into smaller ones.
Being overwhelmed is one of the most frequent causes of poor time management on big projects. If you're feeling overburdened, you might want to put off doing it and focus on something else. Divide big jobs into smaller, more doable chores to get past this feeling.

It is simpler to begin by focusing on individual components of the jigsaw rather than the entire image.

You will make progress and enhance your general time management skills as you work on the project in manageable chunks.

4. Minimize interruptions

Everyone becomes sidetracked. Numerous factors have the potential to impede your development, including emails, social media, coworkers, children, and odd thoughts. It's important to make a concerted effort to reduce the amount of distractions, even when you can't avoid them entirely.

Self-reflection on time management: Determine what is causing you distractions and devise a plan to reduce them. Does your phone need to be in the other room? Is it wise to disable email and text alerts? Does your work computer need to have social media blocked?

5. Put the emails away for later.

Unexpectedly, email can be a time waster. You are destroying your productivity every time you put down what you're doing to check your email.

Transitioning between tasks requires mental effort and time. You can either wait to read your email till after you've completed your present task or set aside a specified time each day to do so.

6. Divide up your time.

By batching your time, you can further leverage the efficiency of not switching jobs. Try to complete any related projects you have at the same time.

You may complete these jobs fast by grouping them together and saving your mental and physical energy for transitioning to a new work. This is a time management strategy that works for any sector or type of work.

7. Cut down on multitasking

Many studies indicate that multitasking reduces productivity, even though it may feel like you are getting more done on your to-do list. Similarly, concentrating on one project at a time would prevent the mental strain of switching between projects, which causes a lag.

Wait and finish the task at hand before going on to the next on your list if you want to make better use of your time.

8. Put vacation time aside on your calendar.

You may save time by organizing all of your activities, meetings, due dates, and assignments on your calendar. Time is saved by having a single location to check these items. Scheduling time can be even more effectively done with online calendar tools like.

The efficacy of this time management technique is increased by the ability to create reminders and see your calendar on several devices.

9. Recognize when to decline meetings

It's not always the best use of time to hold meetings. It can be a good idea to decline if the amount of meetings you have keeps increasing. It could be more beneficial to explain your hectic schedule and request that the meeting be replaced by email instead.

10. Review and summarize your day.

It's time to take stock of your accomplishments at the end of the day and prepare yourself for success the next. Reviewing your list of things to do from that day is a great way to see what you completed and what has to be done tomorrow.

You can also take this opportunity to honestly evaluate how well you handled your time during the day in your end-of-day review. You can determine what's working and where you still need to grow by reflecting on yourself.

Using Technological Tools to Increase Productivity:

Increasing focus and concentration can be facilitated by technology. A variety of software and apps are available to assist people in tracking their progress, blocking distracting websites, and maintaining organization. People can maximize productivity and streamline their workflow by utilizing technology tools.

Practice tasks:

Try creating to-do lists and project deadlines using productivity applications such as Asana or Trello. These tools can assist you in efficiently prioritizing jobs and visualizing your workload.

When working, use browser extensions like Freedom or StayFocusd to prevent access to social media and other distracting websites.

Use time-tracking applications like RescueTime to keep an eye on your online activities and pinpoint areas where your productivity practices need work.

~STRATEGY 6~

Building Energy & Motivation

• Our Greatest Sleep Advice

We examine in more detail how modifying your daily well-being, sleep schedule, and bedroom setting might facilitate sound sleep at night and promote restful wakefulness. There is research behind every habit we emphasize, regardless of how big or little the suggested alteration to your daily schedule is.

Although most people want to sleep better, there are a variety of reasons why they might not be getting enough sleep. You may create a customized sleep regimen that works for your lifestyle with the help of these recommendations.

- **Everyday Health**

Your nighttime sleep can be impacted by your daytime activities. These wellness suggestions center on day-to-day tasks, such as meal planning and scheduling time for outdoor activities.

"Spend a minimum of thirty minutes outside in the daylight."

Why it matters: Your body's circadian rhythm is influenced by natural light, and this has a direct impact on when you feel drowsy. It can be simpler to fall asleep at night if you are exposed to daylight early in the day.

What you can do: Whether it's for your morning coffee or as part of your commute, get outside as early as possible. Opening the windows to let in natural light might also be beneficial. Try to get outside for at least thirty minutes every day.

Every day, go to bed and wake up at the same times. **Why it matters**: Regular sleep has been associated with better sleep, and the time of regular activities like meals might affect sleep cycles.

What you can do is establish a regular wake-up time and follow the same schedule every day. Maintain consistent meal timings for breakfast, lunch, and dinner each day. Have a regular bedtime ritual to cap off your day.

A 20-minute snooze in the early afternoon is the maximum.

Why it matters: Taking a nap in the late afternoon or evening can help you feel less exhausted at night, which could make it more difficult for you to fall asleep.

What you can do is plan a nap for at least eight hours before bedtime and restrict it to no more than twenty minutes.

Add fruits, veggies, and healthy grains to your diet to make it better.

<u>**Why it matters**</u>: Research has linked diet to sleep quality, and vitamins and nutrients allow the body to operate as intended. Improved sleep health may be facilitated by a diet rich in fruits, vegetables, whole grains, and lean meats.

What you can do is discuss your current diet and ways it could be improved with your doctor or a nutritionist, as everyone has different needs.
Use deep breathing and imagery to help you relax.

Why it matters: Depending on how you handle stressful situations, they may or may not interfere with your ability to sleep. Acquiring relaxation skills can increase resilience and lessen the negative effects of stress on sleep.

What you can do is try out several techniques for relaxation, such as deep breathing and visualization, and discover which ones suit you the most. It will be easier for you to employ these strategies at bedtime if you practice them during the day.

- **Sleep Schedule**

The way you sleep has an impact on how well you sleep. Establishing a sound sleep schedule each night helps provide the groundwork for more reliable and peaceful sleep.

Every night, try to get seven hours of sleep.

Why it matters: Sleeping for a minimum of seven hours per night is critical to general health and wellbeing. A packed calendar of events can reduce the amount of time allotted for sleep. You will undoubtedly wind up with insufficient sleep if you do not set aside enough time for relaxation.

What you can do: To determine your ideal sleep and wake periods, utilize a sleep calculator. If you need to get more sleep, move your bedtime later in the day. Try adjusting your schedule by 15 to 30 minutes each night until you get to your ideal bedtime.

Every night, stick to the same pre-bedtime routine.

Why it matters: Your body and mind can be alerted that it is almost time for sleep if you follow the same routine for getting ready for bed. You should feel more prepared for bed after your regimen.

What you can do is modify your evening schedule to fit your individual requirements and inclinations. It could be a good idea to put on some cozy jammies, clean your teeth, engage in some soothing activities, and then turn out the lights. Every night, finish your routine in the same sequence.

Engage in relaxing activities to lessen stress.
Why it matters: Reducing stress can aid in body and mind relaxation, facilitating a peaceful sleep transition. If you wake up throughout the night, it

could be simpler to fall back asleep if you know how to relax your thoughts.

What you can do: Deep breathing, journaling, stretching, reading, meditating, or relaxing to soothing music are common methods of stress relief. To discover the perfect fit, you might need to attempt a few different hobbies.

- **You should just sleep and have sex in bed.**

Why it matters: Establishing a strong mental association between going to bed and sleeping can be beneficial. An excessive amount of time spent awake in bed can exacerbate sleep issues.

What you can do is generally reserve your bed for sleeping and intimate moments. Wait until you are truly exhausted before going to bed each night, and avoid eating, watching TV, studying, and working in bed.

If, after 20 minutes, you are still not asleep, get out of bed.

Why it matters: Constantly tossing and turning in bed might cause annoyance and create a negative relationship between sleeping and being in bed.

What you can do is get out of bed and engage in a relaxing activity if you have been in bed for twenty to thirty minutes without falling asleep. Turn off the lights, stay away from electronics, and go back to bed as soon as you start to nod off.

- **Put your phone on silence**.

Why it matters: Distracting noise and vibrations from phone calls, texts, and other notifications might keep you from sleeping.

What you can do is try to avoid using phones and iPads in the bedroom at all. Put your phone on "**do not disturb**" mode at night to block off notifications if you must have it in the room while you sleep.

Do not look at the time.

Why it matters: It can be more difficult to fall asleep and cause anxiety when one is staring at a clock.

One possible solution is to avoid placing your phone or alarm clock directly next to your bed. Keep them hidden so you won't be tempted to check the clock during the evening.

- **Ambience for Sleep**

By focusing on making your bedroom as comfortable as possible, you may create an environment that encourages restful, uninterrupted sleep.

- **Cut down on or eliminate noise.**

Why it matters: Sleeping in a peaceful atmosphere is preferable. A noisy environment can hinder the quality of your sleep, make it difficult to fall asleep, and create unwelcome awakenings.

What you can do is try blocking out distracting noises with white noise machines or earplugs.

Maintain darkness in the bedroom.

Why it matters: Sleeping soundly is simpler in a bedroom that is dark. Light exposure at night has been linked to shorter sleep and an increased risk of awakening accidentally.

What you can do is use blackout curtains to block out light from the outside and turn out the lights to make your bedroom as dark as possible. Use a sleep mask if you are unable to keep light from entering your bedroom.

- **A temperature of 65 to 68 degrees Fahrenheit should be chosen for your bedroom.**

Why it matters: If your bedroom is too hot or too chilly, you run the risk of having sleep disturbances. The optimal temperature range for a bedroom is typically 65 to 68 degrees Fahrenheit.

What you can do is adjust the thermostat, if you have one, to a setting that suits you. Make strategic use of numerous layers of bedding that you may add or remove as needed to help you stay warm or cool.

- **Make use of a cozy and supportive mattress.**

Why it matters: A comfortable and supportive mattress is essential to a sleep-friendly bedroom because it gives your body the support and comfort it needs.

What you can do: You might want to think about getting a new mattress if your current one is older. A mattress topper can also help you customize the comfort level of your bed.

6.2. Eating for Brain Health

Providing Energy for Your Mental Wonder

The human brain is a powerful organ that controls everything from intricate thoughts to the rhythm of your breathing. It is continuously beeping with electrical signals. However, for optimal performance, your brain need the proper fuel, just like a high-performance automobile. That's the role that nutrition plays!

Refueling Your Attention:
The way your brain works affects how well it can concentrate, learn, and retain information. This is how a well-balanced diet may become the greatest ally for your brain:

A Rainbow on Your Plate: Rich in antioxidants, fruits and vegetables protect brain cells from the damaging effects of free radicals. Imagine them as little barriers defending your superhuman cognitive abilities!

Whole Grains for Steady Energy: Instead of consuming refined carbohydrates, go to whole grains like quinoa and brown rice. They give you a steady stream of energy that keeps your mind active all day long—goodbye afternoon slumps!
Building Blocks: Building and repairing brain cells require protein, which is found in lean protein.

Fish, legumes, and lean meats are all great ways to keep your mind functioning at peak efficiency.

Good Fats for Mental Clarity: Don't be afraid of fat in general!

Avocados and fatty salmon are good sources of healthy fats that are essential for brain cell membrane construction and cognitive function.

How to Outwit Sugar Crashers:

After indulging in sugary delights, many of us have encountered the dreaded sugar crash - a decrease in energy and concentration. To ensure that your mind is working at full capacity, avoid the following:

Sugar Overload: Consuming too much sugar can cause blood sugar levels to fluctuate, which can cause mood swings and make it difficult to focus. Give it some thought before grabbing that sugar bar!

Processed Food Danger: Processed foods frequently contain high levels of added sugars, sodium, and harmful fats. These may exacerbate inflammatory responses in the body, which may have negative effects on brain function. When possible, choose entire, unprocessed meals.

6.3. Overcoming Your Dreams

Creating Realistic Objectives, Step-by-Step
Have you ever been intimidated by a lofty objective, such as learning a new language or finishing a marathon? The majority of us have! That's why it's important to create attainable goals.

These serve as kind of stepping stones to assist you get to where you want to go without making you feel like you're drowning in "to-dos."

Here's how to turn that grand vision into manageable goals you can really achieve:

1. Slice and Dice: Visualize your enormous objective as a gigantic pizza. I mean, you wouldn't try to eat it whole? Slice it instead of cooking it whole. Apply this to your objectives as well! Divide it up into smaller, easier-to-manage activities. If your objective is to run a marathon, for instance, you could set smaller goals like jogging a mile, then two, and so forth.

2. Appreciate the Little Victories: Consider yourself a superhero! You've won a little victory each time you finish a minor assignment. Give yourself a pat on the back, dance joyfully, and indulge in a tiny treat! Honoring these victories helps you stay inspired and serves as a constant reminder that you are improving.

3. Be Sincere with Yourself: It's important to have reasonable goals. Don't expect to become a marathon runner over night from a couch potato. Tell the truth about the amount of time and energy you can actually commit to achieving your objective. You'll be less likely to give up and become disheartened in this way.

4. Adapt as You Go: Sometimes life deals you a curveball. Perhaps you become ill or something unforeseen occurs. That's alright! If necessary, don't be hesitant to modify your deadlines or goals. Recall that progress, not perfection, is what matters.

The Main Idea: Making a road plan for your dreams is similar to setting attainable goals. You can maintain your motivation and keep going forward by starting with tiny, attainable steps and acknowledging your accomplishments along the way.

This strategy will enable you to accomplish your objectives and feel fantastic while doing so!

~STRATEGY 7~

Enhancing Productivity

7.1. Maximizing Your Day: Enhancing Your Ability to Set Priorities

Imagine that you had a mile-long, massive "to-do" list! Of course, some of the things on that list are far more important than others. Rearranging your list to put the most crucial things at the top and take care of them first is comparable to setting priorities.

This is crucial, for that reason:

Focus on What Matters Most: By determining your top priorities, you can make sure that your limited time and energy are allocated to the things that are truly important to you. This can include finishing an assignment for work on time, getting ready for an exam, or spending quality time with close friends and family.

Set the Important Things as Your Top Priorities: We are all aware that there is never enough time to get everything done on our to-do lists. Setting priorities, however, compels you to attend to the most important matters first. In this manner, tasks will get completed even if you eventually run out of steam.

Feel More Successful: You feel so accomplished when you do those crucial tasks. You are motivated to keep going when you realize that you are making progress on the things that are truly important.

Tell me how you go about allocating your responsibilities, please.

Make a mental inventory of everything you have on your plate, including work responsibilities, personal goals, and errands!

Ask yourself "**Why**?" Think to yourself, "Why is this important?" as you go over your list. Does your job have a deadline? A personal commitment? Determining the "why" behind every work helps determine its priority.

Crucial versus urgent: Not everything important needs to be done right away. Divide the jobs you have to do into two categories: important but not urgent and important but not urgent.

Observe the Tigers Initially: Sort your chores into categories, then prioritize the most important and urgent ones. These are your "tigers," the items that need to be taken care of right now.

Arrange the Tasks That Remain: The less important but still important tasks can wait till later or even on a separate day. Just be sure to set up time on your calendar to do them eventually.

> *How do you determine which activity should be completed first while using IQ brainstorming?*

A) Opt for the easiest task possible.

B) Choose the assignment whose due date is the closest.

C) Select the task that best aligns with your long-term goals.

D) To start, select a task at random.

7.2. Tackle Big Projects by Breaking Them Down Into Handleable, Bite-Sized Parts

Have you ever been faced with a huge assignment that loomed over you like a monster and felt absolutely clueless about where to begin? All of them have! That is the place where analysis becomes powerful.

Let's say that monstrous project is a gigantic Lego set. You wouldn't try building the whole thing all at once, would you? You would join together the smaller components as directed one by one until, suddenly, **hey Courtney**!, you had the finished product.

Here's how to break those intimidating chores up into doable chunks:

The Big Picture Take a deep breath at the start of the endeavor and remind yourself of its ultimate goal. What are you hoping to achieve?

Dissect it: Assume that, at this point, you must chop that project into smaller pieces, in the same way that you would chop veggies for a stew. List all of the significant steps that need to be done to finish the project from point A, where it starts, to point B, where it concludes.

Reduce: Try breaking down your main phases into smaller, more doable tasks once you've determined what they are. The secret is to make these small chores something you can complete in a manageable length of time without becoming overwhelmed.

Small Steps, Large Gains: This tactic works well because it lets you focus on completing one small activity at a time. Every task you do is a mini-win, a little victory that motivates you to keep going.

The Procrastination Monster Is Dead: When a task appears difficult or overwhelming, it's easy to put it off until later (procrastination!). On the other hand, it becomes less frightening and you are more likely to actually start if you break it down into manageable bits.

> **IQ Brainstorming**: Why is it advantageous to break up work into smaller, more manageable portions?

A) To increase the estimated duration of the project

B) To create a comprehensive action plan.

C) To add complexity to the project.

D) Overloading the project with unnecessary duties

7.3. Mastering Technology: Boosting Efficiency with Instruments and Applications

Imagine having a variety of useful tools, such a screwdriver for tightening things, a saw for cutting wood, and a hammer for hammering nails. Apps and productivity tools can be thought of as your digital toolkit! Their goal is to increase productivity and ease the burden of your work.

These digital assistants can help you increase your productivity in the following ways:

Superstars of Organization: Do you think you have an excessive amount of sticky notes and to-do lists? Task management applications may well save your life. You can set deadlines, make to-do lists, and even break up big projects into smaller ones with the use of these tools (see point 7.2!). Think of these as digital post-its that won't disappear!

Time Tamers: The utility of digital calendar apps is greater than that of traditional calendars. You can schedule appointments and reminders in addition to designating specific times for certain tasks. By doing this, you may organize your day more effectively and avoid overscheduling.

Project Powerhouses: Do you work on complex, multifaceted projects? Project management tools are at your disposal! You can collaborate with colleagues, assign projects, track progress, and maintain organization with the aid of these apps. It works much like an in-the-back digital project manager to keep things organized.

Reduce Work, Increase Output: Some time-tracking tools can even track how much time you spend on them. It might actually open your eyes! By keeping track of your time, you can uncover possibilities for progress and concentrate on the things that truly matter.

But there's a catch: Don't utilize the applications too much! The objective is to use technology to simplify your life, not to become a slave to it. Choose a few tools that are appropriate for your needs and learn how to use them well.

The Takeaway: By incorporating productivity tools and software into your everyday routine, you may improve your workflow, free up your mind for more creative tasks, and eventually complete more chores in less time. It's like having a team of virtual assistants working in the background to help you all day!

> **IQ Brainstorming:** What are the benefits of utilizing productivity tools and applications?

A) An increase in side activities

B) Improved productivity and organization

C) Longer workdays

D) A decrease in output

~STRATEGY 8~

Managing Emotions and Mood Swings

8.1. Taming the Emotional Rollercoaster: Techniques for Managing Your Feelings

We all experience emotions – joy, sadness, anger, frustration – it's a normal part of life. But sometimes, those emotions can feel overwhelming, like you're on a wild rollercoaster ride with no control.

That's where emotional regulation techniques come in. These are like tools you can use to manage your feelings in a healthy way.

- ***Here are some powerful techniques to add to your emotional toolkit:***

Deep Breaths for the Win: Feeling stressed or overwhelmed? Take a deep breath (or five!). Deep breathing helps activate your body's relaxation response, calming you down and giving you a chance to think clearly before reacting.

Mindfulness Magic: Mindfulness meditation is all about focusing on the present moment. It can help you become more aware of your emotions without getting swept away by them. Imagine your emotions as waves in the ocean – you can see them coming, but you don't have to get caught in the current.

Journaling Journey: Sometimes, just putting pen to paper can be incredibly helpful. Try journaling about your emotions. Writing it down can help you understand them better and identify any triggers that might be setting you off.

Reframing Your Thoughts: Our thoughts can have a big impact on how we feel. Cognitive reframing is a technique where you challenge negative thoughts and replace them with more positive or realistic ones. For example, instead of thinking **"I'm a failure,"** you could reframe it to *"This is a setback, but I can learn from it and try again."*

Practice Makes Progress: Just like learning any new skill, mastering emotional regulation takes time and practice. The more you use these techniques, the better you'll become at managing your emotions in a healthy way. Remember, it's okay to not be perfect.

Be patient with yourself and celebrate your progress along the way. By taking control of your emotions, you'll be better equipped to navigate life's ups and downs and live a more fulfilling life.

> ➤ **IQ Brainstorming:** How does deep breathing help regulate emotions?

A) By increasing heart rate

B) By activating the body's relaxation response

C) By inducing panic attacks

D) By stimulating the sympathetic nervous system

8.2. When to Call in the Emotional Backup: Seeking Professional Help

Sometimes, life throws emotional curveballs that feel impossible to handle on your own. Maybe your mood swings are becoming severe, or you're struggling to cope with difficult emotions. That's when seeking professional help from a therapist, counselor, or mental health professional becomes crucial.

Think of these professionals as emotional trainers. They can provide the guidance, tools, and support you need to develop healthy coping mechanisms and improve your overall emotional well-being. ***Here's why therapy can be a powerful tool:***

Safe Space to Explore: Therapy offers a safe and confidential space where you can openly explore your emotions without judgment. Talking through your struggles with a trained professional can be incredibly helpful in understanding yourself better.

Uncovering the Roots: There might be underlying issues contributing to your emotional difficulties. A therapist can help you identify these issues and develop strategies to address them. For example, if you're struggling with anger, there could be unresolved past experiences that are fueling those emotions.

Building Your Toolkit: Therapy isn't just about talking. Therapists can teach you specific techniques to manage your emotions, like relaxation exercises, communication skills, or cognitive-behavioral therapy (CBT). These tools become part of your emotional toolkit, helping you navigate difficult situations more effectively.

Therapy is Not a Sign of Weakness: Asking for help is a sign of strength! It shows that you're invested in your emotional well-being and willing to take steps to feel better. There's no shame in seeking professional help, and it can be incredibly transformative.

Remember: Finding the right therapist is important. Look for someone you feel comfortable talking to and who specializes in areas relevant to your needs. With the right support, you can learn to manage your emotions in a healthy way and live a more fulfilling life.

8.3. Self-Care: Filling Up Your Emotional Toolbox

Imagine your emotional well-being as a car. To run smoothly, it needs regular maintenance, right? That's where self-care comes in. Self-care activities are like filling up your emotional gas tank, giving yourself the energy and resilience to handle life's challenges.

☐ **Here's how self-care keeps your emotional engine running**:

Recharge Your Batteries: Feeling drained and overwhelmed? Self-care activities like getting enough sleep, eating healthy foods, and exercising can help you recharge physically and mentally. Think of them as plugging your car in to recharge the battery!

Nature's Stress Buster: Spending time in nature is a powerful mood booster. Whether it's going for a walk in the park, sitting by a stream, or simply looking at trees outside your window, immersing yourself in nature can help reduce stress and improve your overall well-being.

Do What Makes You Happy: Self-care isn't all about bubble baths and meditation (although those can be great too!). It's also about engaging in activities you genuinely enjoy, like reading, painting, playing music, or spending time with loved ones. Doing things you find fun helps you relax, de-stress, and feel happy.

Stronger Together: Social connection is crucial for emotional health. Make time for friends, family, or anyone who makes you feel good and supported. Talking to loved ones, laughing together, or simply being around people who care can be incredibly uplifting.

Remember: Self-care isn't selfish, it's essential! By taking care of yourself, you'll be better equipped to handle stress, regulate your emotions, and live a more fulfilling life. There's no right or wrong way to practice self-care.

Find activities that work for you and make them a regular part of your routine. Just like a car needs regular maintenance to run smoothly, your emotional well-being needs self-care to thrive!

> **IQ Brainstorming**: Why is practicing self-care important for managing emotions and mood swings?

A) Because it's a waste of time

B) Because it helps individuals recharge and relax

C) Because it increases stress levels

D) Because it promotes emotional instability

~STRATEGY 9~

Strengthening Relationships

9.1 Successful Communication Techniques:
Healthy relationships are built on efficient communication. It requires gently and clearly articulating requirements, goals, and viewpoints.

Talk It Out: Powerful Communication Techniques for Sturdy Partnerships
Like a bridge, speech ties you to other individuals. It lets you to convey your needs, wants, and thoughts to others around you.

But miscommunications can arise and that bridge can become fragile at times. The following communication skills can help you develop enduring and positive relationships:

"I" Statements for the Win: Try adopting "I" statements in place of finger-pointing and attributing responsibility to others (or saying "you always"). "I" words assist focus on how you feel and what you need, without casting blame on the other person.

For instance, consider expressing "I feel frustrated when the dishes are left out because I have to clean them up," instead of "You make me so mad when you leave your dirty dishes everywhere."

Putting Oneself in Their Shoes: Make an attempt to understand other people's viewpoints. We call this empathy. Understanding their point of view will help you communicate more effectively and eliminate misunderstandings. Ask yourself, **"How might they be feeling?"**

Being assertive requires expressing yourself in a courteous yet clear and confident manner. It has nothing to do with shouting or behaving aggressive. Talk about what's upsetting you in a clear, calm manner. Say, "I would like to talk about something that's been upsetting me," as an example.

Keep in mind that discourse is two-way:
Active listening goes beyond merely hearing what someone is saying. It's vital to observe their overall message, tone of voice, and body language. To signal that you are interested in the conversation, make eye contact, nod your head, and ask clarifying questions.

Being open and sincere is vital in relationships. Openly and honestly discuss your thoughts and feelings, but careful how you say it (this is where assertiveness and "I" statements come in helpful).

By implementing these tips, you can build effective communication skills that will enable you to establish more meaningful connections with people, handle issues amicably, and forge durable bonds.

Therefore, keep these communication skills in mind the next time you need to discuss something; they will serve as your bridge to a deeper comprehension!

> **Brainstorming on Intelligence:** What makes "I" statements valuable in communication?

A) Because they transfer the emphasis from fault to subjective feelings

B) Because they make the listener more protective

C) Since they encourage miscommunication

D) Because they emphasize understanding above criticism

9.2. The Effectiveness of Active Listening to Actually Hear Someone

Ever find yourself speaking with a brick wall? Even when you seem to be giving everything you have, the other person seems to be miles away. Active listening can help with it. It's similar like donning specialist headphones for hearing that enable you to fully absorb the words and emotions of the other person.

Here's why establishing amazing relationships through attentive listening works like magic:

Putting your phone away, staring the speaker in the eye, and focussing entirely on them are all part of offering your whole attention. It conveys to them your interest in their opinions.

Active listening is more than just hearing what is being said; it goes beyond that. It involves seeking to interpret the feelings that underlying those words. Observe their facial expressions, body language, and tone of voice.

Paying Attention, Not Distracted: Avoid formulating your response during the other person's speech. This suggests that you're not paying attention. Rather, aim to stay in the present and take in what they are saying.

Mirroring and Summarizing: If you occasionally mirror what the other person is saying or summarize what you've heard, you can show them that you're paying attention. One alternative reaction may be to say something like, "*So what you're saying is...*" or "It sounds like you're feeling frustrated."

It's a gift to actively listen:
Someone may tell you care for them when you listen to them closely. People feel heard and respected, and bonds are reinforced as a result of it. This is particularly important when trying to settle disagreements or just have more in-depth, meaningful conversations.

> ➤ **IQ Brainstorming**: What is active listening's major objective?

~89~

A) To control the conversation

B) To exhibit compassion and understanding

C) To disagree with the speaker's point of view

D) Disregarding the speaker's emotions

9.3. **Handling Tension:** Dispute Settlement Methods for More Robust Connections

It's a reality that disputes exist in all relationships. Perhaps it's with a family member, friend, or even a love relationship. The good news is that those relationships don't have to be ruined by disagreement. In fact, it can strengthen them if managed appropriately! Here are some ideas for turn those arguments into learning opportunities:

The Power of Listening: A returning favorite! A major component of dispute resolution is active listening (see point 9.2). It conveys to the other person your respect for their position and your wish to learn more about it.

Finding Common Ground: There are frequently moments of agreement even in the thick of disagreements. Concentrate on the area of agreement! This may help to diffuse tension in the debate and encourage problem-solving.

The answer is to compromise: nobody is ever able to obtain all they wish. Compromise is often at the center of dispute resolution. See whether the other person is prepared to adjust slightly as well.

Empathy Avenue: Make an attempt to understand other people's views. This can assist you in understanding their perspective, but it doesn't imply you have to agree with them. To observe things from their viewpoint, try spending some time wandering along their street.

Communicate Openly and Honestly: Hiding your feelings will only intensify the situation.

Remember to be courteous as you share your feelings in an honest and open manner. In this scenario, "I" statements (see point 9.1) can be useful.

Recall that there are two sides to every conflict. It is vital for all sides to be willing to listen, make concessions, and adopt an open-minded approach to the matter.

The Aftermath: After the disagreement has been settled, give it some thought. What else might you have done? What did you discover? You may establish healthier, more resilient relationships in the future by adopting the lessons you learn from every disagreement.

> ➤ **IQ Brainstorming:** What is compromise vital to settling conflicts?

A) Since it guarantees that one party will acquire what they seek

B)   Since   it   develops   cooperation   and comprehension

C) Since it intensifies disputes

D) Since it evades dealing with the core concerns

~STRATEGY 10~

Maintaining a Balanced Lifestyle

10. Striking a Balance Between Work and Life

Finding harmony in a multitude of areas of life, including career, relationships, hobbies, and health, is crucial to leading a balanced existence. This equilibrium promotes life satisfaction, lowers stress levels, and improves general well-being.

10.1. Discovering Your Sweet Spot: *Balancing Work and Life to Be Happy*

Consider life as a huge pie. You want to save some for friends and family, some for work, some for sleep, and some for hobbies. However, on occasion, it appears as though the labor slice is swallowing the entire pie! Work-life balance then becomes crucial. It's about allocating a decent amount of time and effort to each aspect of your life.

> **Work-life balance is vital for the following reasons;**

Preventing Burnout City: Burnout, or the feeling of being fully exhausted, can arise from work taking over your life. It's possible that you're worn out, nervous, and shut off from everything important. Maintaining a work-life balance allows you to take breaks and refresh, which helps you avoid burnout.

Work is crucial, but it's not everything.

Happy Mind, Happy Life. You stay happy and psychologically well when you make time for hobbies, quality time with loved ones, and relaxation outside of work.

More Productive You: It may surprise you to hear that taking breaks and keeping a personal life might enhance your productivity at work! You may concentrate more successfully and complete more activities during work hours when you're well-rested and invigorated.

> **Discovering your optimum work-life balance includes the following critical components**

Establishing Boundaries: This means recognizing when to say no to additional work, particularly when it begins to eat up your spare time. It's acceptable to establish limitations and defend your own time.

Setting Priorities Like a Pro: Not every task at work is made equal. Acquire the art of prioritizing what matters most and allocating or doing away with less important activities. Time for the things that really matter is freed up as a result.

Creating Time for Fun: Just like you would for a work meeting, arrange time for enjoyable activities! Make time for your personal life just like you would a crucial appointment; schedule it and keep to it.

Remember: Achieving a perfect 50/50 split isn't the goal of work-life balance. It's all about figuring out what suits you. It's acceptable if job takes more of your concentrate on some days. To make sure that every part of your life receives the attention it need, the answer is to practice awareness and to change as necessary.

You're investing in your overall well-being and preparing yourself for a happier, more fulfilling life when you build a healthy work-life balance!

Practice Exercise: Make a weekly schedule with precise times allowed for work, recreation, fitness, and socializing. As much as you can, follow this timetable, and assess how efficiently it benefits you in attaining fulfillment and balance in your life.

> ➤ **IQ Brainstorming**: What conceivable ramifications might neglecting work-life balance have?

A) Enhanced output

B) Better mental well-being

C) Decreased job satisfaction and burnout

D) Increased inventiveness

10.2. Putting Up Your Own Wall: *The Influence of Limits*

Consider that your life is a magnificent garden. While you want people to enjoy it, keeping a healthy environment also demands a fence. Limits mirror that fence. They support you in safeguarding your relationships' wellbeing, time, and energy.

Here's why establishing boundaries is crucial:

Healthy Relationships: By laying down clear expectations, limits encourage healthy relationships. People are aware of your expectations of them and vice versa. This lowers anger and confusion.

Respect Your Time: Effective time management demands setting boundaries. You can have more time for yourself and the things that are important to you by decreasing your working hours or declining additional obligations.

Stop the Drain: People can suck your energy if you don't set limits. Perhaps a family member stays too long or a friend asks for favors all the time. By etiquettely communicating your constraints, boundaries help avert this.

So, how can one make a durable border fence?

Know Your boundaries: Determining your boundaries is the first step. How much time are you able to spend working? Which habits are uncomfortable for you?

Communication is Key: Once you are aware of your boundaries, let people know about them in a calm

and direct manner. "I value our time together, but evenings are for me to relax. Can we meet up on weekends?" is one example of what you could say.
Adhering to Your Principles: Occasionally, someone may push your bounds.

That's alright! Adopt a firm attitude and honor your promise. Sayings like "I know you're disappointed, but this is what works for me" are suitable.
Recall that having boundaries does not equate being selfish or nasty.

They are about ensuring your wellbeing and maintaining your dignity. Respect for one another's boundaries is a core part of effective relationships.

You may construct a more secure and supportive environment for yourself as well as deeper, more enjoyable interactions with others by setting and enforcing healthy limits.

Practice Exercise: List the occasions in your life where you believe that your rights aren't being upheld or where you find it difficult to stand up for yourself. In these scenarios, try saying "no" or assertively expressing your wants. Then, notice how it improves your sense of empowerment and wellbeing.

> **IQ Brainstorming:** Why do relationships need boundaries?

A) Since they divide people from one another

B) Since they develop understanding and respect for one another

C) Since they do away with the demand for discussion

D) Since they foster codependency

Conclusion

Having a balanced lifestyle requires a variety of things, including controlling one's emotions, enhancing productivity, building stronger ties with others, and protecting one's general wellbeing. Every one of these factors is vital to living a happy and fulfilling life.

People can notice big improvements in their daily lives by putting the techniques taught in this series into practice. These strategies, which range from maintaining a distraction-free atmosphere to prioritizing work and defining realistic goals, are supposed to promote emotional stability, productivity, and attentiveness.

In addition, people can cement their relationships and establish a network of friends and family that supports them by prioritizing effective communication and conflict resolution, practicing self-care, and receiving professional assistance when necessary.

Setting limits and achieving a healthy work-life balance are vital to preventing burnout and sustaining harmony in both the personal and professional worlds.

In the end, achieving a balanced lifestyle is a constant process that asks for determination, introspection, and adaptability. People can start along the path to increased resilience, pleasure, and contentment by integrating these concepts into their daily routines.

I strongly suggest readers to look into the other series of this book in order to obtain greater insight and understanding of these themes. Readers seeking a more balanced and fulfilled existence will find helpful exercises, ideas, and advice in every area. Order the full series now to move forward in your own development!

THANKS FOR READING THE 1ST SERIES, YOU CAN GET MORE BOOKS FROM MY AUTHOR CENTRAL PAGE